Let's
Immigration

Collecting Data

Spencer Toole

COMPUTER SCIENCE For the REAL World™

Rosen Classroom™

Published in 2018 by The Rosen Publishing Group, Inc.
29 East 21st Street, New York, NY 10010

Book Design: Jennifer Ryder-Talbot
Editor: Caitie McAneney

Photo Credits: Cover GagliardiImages/
Shutterstock.com; p. 4-5, 10-11, 12-13, 14, 18-19 Everett Historical/
Shutterstock.com; p. 4, 8, 12, 16, 20 (Statue of Liberty icon) Mariya Isachenko/
Shutterstock.com; p. 6-7 Victoria Lipov/
Shutterstock.com; p. 6, 10, 14, 18, 22 (American flag icon) Joe Belanger/
Shutterstock.com; p. 9 Richard Semik/Shutterstock.com; p. 16 PlusONE/
Shutterstock.com; p. 20 Joseph Sohm/Shutterstock.com.

Library of Congress-in-Publication Data

Names: Toole, Spencer.
Title: Let's study immigration: collecting data / Spencer Toole.
Description: New York : Rosen Classroom, 2018. | Series: Computer Kids: Powered by
Computational Thinking | Includes glossary and index.
Identifiers: LCCN ISBN 9781538353165 (pbk.) | ISBN 9781538324073 (library bound) |
ISBN 9781538353233 (6pack) | ISBN 9781508137504 (ebook)
Subjects: LCSH: United States--Emigration and immigration--Juvenile literature. |
Emigration and immigration law--United States--Juvenile literature. | Immigrants--United
States--Juvenile literature.
Classification: LCC KF4819.85 T66 2018 | DDC 325.73--dc23

Manufactured in the United States of America

CPSIA Compliance Information: Batch #WS18RC: For Further Information contact Rosen Publishing, New York, New York at 1-800-237-9932

Table of Contents

What's Immigration?

The United States is a country of immigrants. Most of us have **ancestors** who came from other parts of the world in the last four hundred years. Immigration is moving from one place to another to live **permanently**.

This photograph of Ellis Island was taken nearly one hundred years ago, when the immigration station was still active.

People started keeping detailed records on immigration in the 1800s. Ships recorded information on their passengers. Later, an official immigration station opened up in New York City. It was called Castle Garden. In 1892, a new immigration station opened called Ellis Island.

Ellis Island is near the Statue of Liberty. This statue welcomed immigrants with the promise of freedom.

Ellis Island

Ellis Island is one of the most famous arrival points for immigrants to the United States. It was open as an immigrant processing center from 1892 to 1924. You can visit Ellis Island today to gather information about immigration during that time.

Ellis Island is in New York Harbor. You have to take a ferry, or a boat, to get there. The ferries pass the Statue of Liberty, which was the first thing immigrants saw when they arrived. The statue was a sign of hope for the immigrants.

Ancestry

Millions of people passed through Ellis Island. For that reason, many people can learn about their **ancestry** by looking at data from Ellis Island. If you know your ancestor's name, you can find out where they came from, the day they arrived in the United States, and more.

Officials at Ellis Island collected information from each passenger, and much of it is available today. You can learn about your ancestors online. Many ancestry websites pull information from Ellis Island.

You can visit the Ellis Island National Museum of Immigration today and see how immigrants once entered the United States.

Collecting Data

How did officials at Ellis Island collect data? They didn't have computers like we do today. They had people fill out forms, called "ship passenger arrival records."

When people arrived at Ellis Island, they usually only had a bag or a trunk with all of their belongings.

These records asked immigrants many questions. Immigrants had to record their name, where they were born, their job, and where they lived last. The records also asked about the date they arrived in the United States and the ship on which they arrived. We know a lot about immigrants because of these records!

Welcome to America!

How many people passed through the halls of Ellis Island per day? During its busiest years, between 5,000 and 10,000 people went through the immigration process daily. Ellis Island was very crowded!

Once immigrants were well inspected, they could take a ferry to New York City to start their new lives.

What happened to immigrants when they arrived? First, they had to be **inspected** for medical problems. Some were sent home if they had a **contagious** illness. Those who passed the medical test were then asked **legal** questions. This helped officials both collect data and keep the country safe.

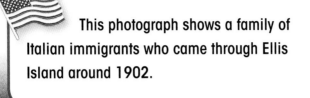

This photograph shows a family of Italian immigrants who came through Ellis Island around 1902.

Nationality

One of the most important pieces of data about immigrants was their nationality. A person's nationality depends on their home country. Data about nationality helps people today find out where their ancestors came from. It also helps **historians** look at patterns of immigration.

For example, from data collected at Ellis Island, we know that many of the first immigrants to come to the United States were from Germany, Russia, Ireland, Italy, and Austria-Hungary. As time went on, more Jewish, Scottish, and Polish people came over, among other nationalities.

This is the main hall of Ellis Island. Millions of people passed through this area during its active years.

How Many Immigrants?

Data from Ellis Island can also show you how many people arrived each year. Some years, there were fewer than 200,000 people. Other years, more than 800,000 people came to the United States.

The first year Ellis Island accepted immigrants was 1892. That year, 445,987 people came through the immigration center. In the years after World War I, fewer than 30,000 people immigrated per year. Ellis Island's busiest year was 1907, when 1,004,756 immigrants came through its processing center.

Immigration Statistics

Data can be related through statistics. Statistics are collections of information that are given in numbers. Some statistics are percentages, or parts of a whole. For example, using data, people estimate that almost 40 percent of Americans today have an ancestor that went through Ellis Island.

Other forms of data include photographs from Ellis Island. You may be able to find a photograph of your ancestors when they arrived!

People also use data to show that more than 12 million immigrants entered the United States through Ellis Island. Statistics like this one are useful because they help people realize the great number of immigrants that have arrived in the United States.

New American citizens must go through a **naturalization** process. This photograph shows a ceremony to celebrate citizens' naturalization.

Today's Immigrants

Do officials still collect data like they did in Ellis Island? Today, officials collect even more detailed data on people entering the United States. They collect information about people who are here **temporarily**, those who are **refugees**, and those who become **permanent residents**.

Let's look at the number of people who become permanent residents per year. In 2015, 1,051,031 people became permanent residents. That's less than in 2005, when 1,122,257 people became permanent residents, but more than in 1995, when 720,177 people became permanent residents.

How Is Data Helpful?

How can immigration data help us? It gives us a look at the number of people who enter our country, or did so in the past. It shows us where people came from, so we know what nationalities make up the American **melting pot**.

Computer programs can take data and make it into graphs and charts. These help people better visualize, or picture, what the data means. You can see the difference in the number of immigrants from one year to the next. Data helps us learn about our country!

Glossary

ancestor: A relative who lived long before you.

ancestry: The line of relatives that have come before you.

contagious: Able to be spread through contact.

historian: A person who studies history.

inspect: To look something over very carefully.

legal: Lawful.

melting pot: A place where many different kinds of cultures, races, or individuals come together into a whole.

naturalization: The granting of citizenship to someone of foreign birth.

permanent resident: Someone who lawfully lives in a country.

permanently: For a long time.

refugee: Someone who is seeking a safe place to live, especially during a time of war.

temporarily: For a short time.

Index